W9-CUP-082

ASCENDING RED CEDAR MOON

*for my friends
among the students
of Immaculate High
Warmest regards,
Duane Niatum
Seattle
March, 1975*

LEARNING RESOURCES CENTER
IMMACULATE HIGH SCHOOL
803 TERRY AVENUE
SEATTLE, WASHINGTON 98104

ASCENDING RED CEDAR MOON

by Duane Niatum

HARPER & ROW, *Publishers*
New York   Evanston   San Francisco
London

LEARNING RESOURCES CENTER
IMMACULATE ~~~~~~~~
803 TERRY AVENJE
SEATTLE, WASHINGTON 98104

Grateful acknowledgement is made to the following magazines in which some of these poems first appeared: American Poetry Review, Argus (Seattle), Assay, BLEB, Choice, Chicago Review, Cimarron Review, Contempora, Greenfield Review, Guabi, The Human Voice, Inscape, Jeopardy, Madrona, The Miscellany, Modine Gunch, Mill Mountain Review, New York Quarterly, Northwest Review, Pembroke, Pendulum, Pequod, Poetry Northwest, Prairie Schooner, Puget Soundings, Quetzal, Scimitar and Song, Spring Rain, South Dakota Review, Tacoma News Tribune, West Coast Poetry Review, World Order.

Anthologies: *An American Indian Anthology,* Blue Cloud Quarterly, 1971; *American Indian II,* University of South Dakota Press, 1971; *From The Belly of The Shark,* Edited by Walter Lowenfels, Random House, 1973; *Come To Power,* Edited by Dick Lourie, Crossing Press, 1973.

Some of these poems appeared originally in a chapbook *Taos Pueblo And Other Poems,* published by Greenfield Review Press, 1973.

Typography and jacket design by Christine Aulicino

ASCENDING RED CEDAR MOON
Copyright © 1969, 1970, 1971, 1972, 1973 by Duane Niatum
All rights reserved. Printed in the United States of America.
No part of this book may be used or reproduced in any manner whatsoever without written permission except in the case of brief quotations embodied in critical articles and reviews. For information address Harper & Row, Publishers, Inc., 10 East 53rd Street, New York, N.Y. 10022

Library of Congress Cataloging in Publication Data

Niatum, Duane, 1938-
Ascending red cedar moon.

I. Title.
PS3564.I17A9   1974   811'.5'4   73-18752

International Standard Book Number: 06-451150-2 (hard cover)
                                                           06-451153-7 (paperback)

FIRST EDITION

*For my friends
and our elder poets*

CONTENTS

I. ASCENDING RED CEDAR MOON

Indian Rock, Bainbridge Island,
    Washington   3

Chief Leschi of the Nisqually   4

No One Remembers Abandoning the Village
    of White Firs   5

Being Turned Around by Yellow Leaf
    Moon   8

On Leaving Baltimore   10

Three Poems for Suzanne   12

The Rhythm   14

Taos Pueblo   16

Poem for the People Who Came from
    the Moon   20

A Basket of Three Avocados   21

Ascending Red Cedar Moon   22

At a Friend's Houseboat   24

Homage to Chagall   26

Elegy for Louise Bogan   27

The Calligraphy of Thought   28

At the First of Four Paths to the
    Hohokam Ruins   30

Poem in December   32

Ode to a Generation   34

Friends at the Lake   36

After Consulting an Elder Poet on an
    Anti-war Poem   38

The Sixties, No. 1   40

The Sixties, No. 2   41

The Sixties, No. 3   42

The Sixties, No. 4   43

Where the Dead Endure, the Living Sing   44

To Your Question   46

Crow's Cottage   47

The Clown   48

The Man Still Chants for Her   50

Elegy for Vernon Watkins   51

For My Friends Living Along the
    Walla Walla River   52

A Journey to Guemes Island in August   54

Love Poem   55

The Talking Walls   56

In Praise of the Dark   58

Slow Dancer That No One Hears
    But You   59

The Open Window   60

To Pain   61

The Storm   62

Poem to Those Now United
    by Cankpe Opi   63

II. LEGENDS OF THE MOON

Center Moon   67

Long Day Moon   68

Sore Eye Moon   69

Frog's Moon   70

Idle Moon   71

Full Leaf Moon   72

Red Berries Moon   73

Black Cherries Moon   74

Yellow Leaf Moon   75

Moon of Changing Seasons   76

Frost Moon   77

Center Moon's Little Brother   78

Moon Names   79

Glossary   80

Songs are thoughts, sung out with the breath when people are moved by great forces and ordinary speech is no longer enough. Man is moved just like the ice floe sailing here and there in the current. His thoughts are driven by a flowing force when he feels joy, when he feels fear, when he feels sorrow. Thoughts can wash over him like a flood, making his breath come in gasps and his heart throb. Something like a break in the weather will keep him thawed up. And then it will happen that we, who always think we are small, will feel still smaller. And we will fear to use words. But it will happen that the words we need will come of themselves. When the words we want to use shoot up of themselves—we get a new song.

—Orpingalik,
Eskimo Shaman
of the Netsilik

I

ASCENDING
RED CEDAR
MOON

Sometimes I go about pitying myself,
And all the time
I am being carried on great winds across the sky.
                                        —Chippewa

INDIAN ROCK, BAINBRIDGE ISLAND, WASHINGTON
(for Mary Randlett)

When you reach to touch the markings
On my face, step from the lodge
Of patience, then listen to the order
Of sand and cedar, totem and fishnet,
Blossom and oyster,
Gulls diving into surfaces,
Green journeys of salmon,
Time sapping the season
Of the red-breasted woodpecker.

When you are as motionless as the crane
In the cattails, breathing like the tide,
Then I will chant the legend
To help you hear the paddles thrust,
The rattling bones, the chattering masks,
Your dead ancestors dancing down the beach.

When the long-leaf rains have chilled
Your bones in the morning gale,
Changed your direction to the cottage,
Your drive to the city,
I will end the whaler's song,
Leaving you alone to bend like the reed.

CHIEF LESCHI OF
THE NISQUALLY

He awoke this morning from a strange dream—
Thunderbird wept for him in the blizzard.
Holding him in their circle, Nisqually women
Turn to the river, dance to its song.

He burned in the forest like a red cedar,
His arms fanning blue flames toward
The white men claiming the camas valley
For their pigs and fowl.
Musing over wolf tracks vanishing in snow,
The memory of his wives and children
Keeps him mute. Flickering in the dawn fires,
His faith grows roots, tricks the soldiers
Like a fawn, sleeping black as the brush.

They laugh at his fate, frozen as a bat
Against his throat. Still, death will take
Him only to his father's longhouse,
Past the flaming rainbow door. These bars
Hold but his tired body; he will eat little
And speak less before he hangs.

❧ *NO ONE REMEMBERS*
ABANDONING THE
VILLAGE OF WHITE FIR

1

As a child of cedar, hemlock, and the sea,
I often slept under totem and star,
Sometimes hanging under the black lids
Of a bat's closed eyes to seal off
My soul from the drone of my mother's wrath.

Time formed itself from rimes of the Elwah,
Rainbow river of my ancestors,
Whose arts were fishing, hunting,
Dance, and occasionally war.
Winds then clacked like bone rattles,
Shaking lost meters from the dark.
Many salmon still swim the rapid dreams
Of those children left alone with bluejay and
        chipmunk.
And when the shaman called to wolf,
I sealed up cave after cave.

2

Dancing back to eagle's nest, our blood sang.
Soon hearing river's morning song,
I followed its shadow into the sky,
Reached the snowy tip of Memp-ch-ton's white wing.
At the summit, wild rose and lupine
Hid like worms from the stone's avalanche.

On other days, I ran through a childhood
Of a dozen myths, seeing the fruit on the tree
In the light of Black Cherries Moon
As memories to be plucked for my escape
From the wreckage of scars.

3

Crawling into the cave of another nightmare,
I was left furless, a bear, clawing
Its way past the hissing, howling blizzard.
Seatco chased me to the edge of my cries.
Coyote tossed me into death's arms.
An old man who appeared in the blackwinged
       passage
Sadly shook his head,
Shamed by my fear, but not my failure.
Grandfather, you and Great-Uncle
Were the only men I have known:
Your spirits have been my shield.
Someday, may I step in the shadow of your courage,
Offer your songs to the children and nameless poor?

4

Figures on the outer sides of baskets
Move quietly through morning;
The women are first to see the sun reach the river.
Hoping to live through the vision,
An Elder awakens to the wrens,
Tosses the moon out for one more night.

5

Spinning on colors of the unfinished meadow,
The earth covers up her past
With a celebration of wind and acorn;
Hears women and children picking
Roots and laughing. Today, these paths disappear
Like hawk, deer, the fern dreamers.
And this eroding wood barely draws the stranger
Into the clearing, the red-bone center of sunrise.

6

Watching for the shifts in the yellow leaf fire,
I seek the glow of a cedar cone in ash,
An offering to burn in the city,
Until I see the face of *O-le-man* smile
Before vanishing in the rainbow,
Motioning me to return to wolf's chant
Round the fire that starts the morning song.

Never quite as constant as the moon,
I speak to the bats once again—
Stop when Trickster calls

       "Niatum!   Niatum!"

LEARNING RESOURCES CENTER
IMMACULATE HIGH SCHOOL
803 TERRY AVENUE
SEATTLE, WASHINGTON 98104

BEING TURNED AROUND BY YELLOW LEAF MOON

1

Night blue as abstract as the ninth
Return of Yellow Leaf Moon—
Crows are flying in fields of river willow,
Slowing life to a complicated new dusk.

Dinner flies call Dreamer to the door;
Walk up and down the screen like planetary ghosts.

On the porch, I am no longer sure the guests
Sound their origins. I offer them water,
Honey, the companionship of a brief Bach cantata,
But nothing more. After dinner,
While reading, I realize one void merely empties
Into the main current, green
And vocal as an allegory of algae.

Ocher lights wander about the room,
Suggesting I let my eyes rest
With the blind, the mute, the vanquished.

2

The white peacock in the window speaks
For a longer silence in the solitude of changing suns,
As if the strangers next door
Had locked their lives, sealed off the music.
With a little effort at crossing the room
I begin to understand my figure in the landscape.

Wind carries the secrets blackbirds toss like acorns;
The coughing, cloudy shadow retreats.

Learning to be buoyant, rhythmical, humble as a
      reed
Is what scarecrow calls earth's yellow meditation.

Here within the circle I sing by the totems
Of my ancestors; sleep before I speak
To my love of stepping on the yellow leaves
Down the street, harvesting patterns,
Before the next moon lets me go, and opens.

❧ *ON LEAVING BALTIMORE*

1

Memory pales in the face of the moon,
Shedding it like a skin.
Silence opens the window, the door, the mirror.
Condemning all to the teeth,
It steps into the street everyone's heard tear
Owl from the oak, scanning the field.

2

A falling star heaves the word against the wall.
Dodging this way, then that, I hope
The wind stays lost in history.
That damn owl. For years I've been waiting
For it to speak up, announce the dream is a fraud,
Send the insomniac back to the bed
That haunts him like a bat.

3

A weary stone drags its way toward the river.
Wanting to say I understand,
Ask if it needs a hand, but before I can speak,
Owl swoops down, drowning my voice.

4

If a god is around, he, she, or it must wonder
What link snapped when death suddenly gasped,
Choked, then kept on chanting. Now the only
        fugitives
That see hope alone are the alders,
Happy as winds put storm away to sleep.
Their roots burrow like moles beneath the swamp.

5

Parading along the crevice of my eye, forever
Doing its eight-legged dance,
Spider starts the long trek through the doors,
The windows, the mirror, off to the hills, mud.
Exhausted, everyone watches for time
To shake like a skeleton. Even the mountains
Hail the avalanche of sand and sea,
Bursting from the rip in the sun.

❧ THREE POEMS FOR SUZANNE

1

Tonight, the inlet wind turns birch
Leaves to barnacles. Camas Moon grows cold,
Dying again for the sea. Even the gulls

Are crests on the pilings, so easily settling
Down to roost in the pupils of his mind:
Spirit offerings to his returning shadow.

Along the beach, he thinks of a letter he may
Never write. And love poems are as incomplete
As mythology, never naked as the sun, sand,

Their hot skin. His desire now empties itself
Of her collapsing anguish, his vow
To remain passive. Apart from his yellow feelings,

He wonders if she'll ever live with storms?
Still, one morning will he hear her calling him?

2

Is she seeing herself as the mirror?
Is her soul dancing on this side of the window
With the swallow-tailed butterfly, praying?

Sitting in the prism of her breathing,
Has the sun opened her eyes to river woman,
Reaching the spiral pine hills?

Has she heard the stone calling?
Bathed the wounds in the hourless lake?
Walked in the field of the flaming peacocks?

3

Last night's dream closes the door:
Yellow stems are counting on the stars, voicing
     dawn.
She leaves her home, barefoot.

Stopping at the door, she blows a kiss
Once to the girl, tugging at her father's coat.
The child's tears fall like shattered glass

At her feet, yet, she's steady, not surprised.
Outside, the sparrows are whispering their
     allegiances,
Accenting the pulsing emptiness of the street.

A fear nearly drives her into her mother's room,
But now seeing her first vision of solitude,
She moves on into silence, into dance.

✣ THE RHYTHM

Stone in
The air
Skips on
The sound
Of water;
In my ears,
The falls
Of sunset.

Woman at
My side,
Her body
Swims in
My shadow,
And mine
In hers;
We hear
The river
Call us
Closer.

Village
Animals run
On Changer's
Tracks at
The mouth
Of Nooksack
River.

Mount Komo
Kulshan
Carves
Bluejay
To the
Pinebranch,
Light keeper
Of acorn
And moon.

Lummi show
Us how
To dance
Like fern
And willow,
Love like
The earth
And sky.

❧ *TAOS PUEBLO*

1   IN THE DUST OF THE VALLEY

Bringing my mind to rest in the Pueblo sun,
I let it sink into the sand
Like a turquoise knife. A hawk circles
The powder-blue sky. Crows chant
In the tongue of drifting dust,
If I sit among stones, and listen.

The space of the valley reflects
A hard-edge picture for me, the stranger.
My old paintings of this aspen grove
Are vanishing faces of coyote.
Only hawk's eye looms higher than the mountain.
With each step forward, the voices
From the water drum settle the mood
Of life and death over man and beast,
When each soul matches heart for heart.

The rippling stream divides the Pueblo
Into two villages of the sun,
And like sound without echo, flows
Through the valley and plunges underground.
White buffalo bury our prayers in the clay.

Taos medicine men with painted masks
Discovered in ancient times the mind of rain
Grows in the cactus of sand:
The whole plant, from root to spine is holy,
To be honored like a child or an old mother.
The emerging dreamer untangles himself
In the light blossoming through the plaza;
His cry rattles skyward to meet the sun.

Holding my breath and closing my eyes,
I read the sunspots on my eyelids:
An orange mosaic waterfall.

Under the broad shadow of the mountain,
I feel my son's notebook may
Recreate in cedar the memories of this place
If the children will call him old friend
From the north of their song.

Loving the Kachina dances and the rose
Of poetry, he will feel no fear
At the foot of the mountain. For neither he
Nor the mountain can fly like the hawk.

Speaking to me as a son, the Elders say
I must see the Pueblo's river is sacred
And accessible. Then, I am welcome at Taos.

2   MOUNT TAOS
Carved out of sky, ridges of eagle's field
Hang Pueblo history above Blue Lake.
Adobe houses cluster below,
The blood of brown bodies flows with wind
Down the mesa. Dust reddens in the sun
With the footprints of pilgrims.
The lake water cools their thirst,
Returns their black eyes to the earth.

3   IN THE VILLAGE OF TAOS
An old man with burro tramples
Away the empty street in the noon silence.
A blue lizard rolls his tongue out
To catch a fly: one more god of light.

White and yellow corn plants are rooted
To the rhythms of the women's feet.
With his load of chopped and packed wood,
The burro marks a legend with hoofs
That ring like bells. What must the old
Man have thought a thousand years ago?
Was the sun as dark-red as the man?

Filling the day with a coyote sunset,
The joy of their toil returns to the river.
The gates of the village open early
For the humble man; open often to his retreat.

4   THE GHOSTS

By evening, the eyes of hawk darken.
They have scanned the sagebrush and red willows
For running animals all afternoon.
He will soon break into shadow.
The shriek of this bird lives long after
The face and the flight are forgotten.

5   THE DANCE

Women leaning from small doorways
Begin to sway toward the fiesta in the square.
In the companionship of adobe dreams,
The Elders doze. The old men when awake
Have alert eyes, suspicious, never laughing.
In the square, full-bosomed brownskinned girls
Laugh with the children in the windows,
Thin roots from the earth's crust.
Holding the unconquerable red dust from earth's
Core, the Elders toss it daily
To the spirits on Mount Taos.

6 CHOKE CHERRIES, PLUM BLOSSOMS, THE HEART OF SAND

Drawing Pueblo memories for children awaking,
Kachina winds weave through cornstalks.
The cactus flowers into a dark-orange valley.
Red stallions cross the mountain river
Toward the village in honor of First People.
Crickets enter the silence of stars,
Leaving the young with a blood-red morning.

Whispering the mystery of Taos,
Moon Woman sings to the mesa sleepers.
Their strength whirls in the dust.
In the zig-zag fields, the sorrows of these
Women wander back to their black-winged
     shadows.

7 THE DAWN

Slowly, the light scent of plum blossoms
Pass through the rooms: each window
Mirrors the turquoise mountain, the hawk's circle.

The village children shake me gently from sleep,
Call me to breakfast in the Pueblo.
When they skip off to play, listen for blackbirds
And insects evolving the day, I turn
To Mount Taos—hope my son will visit
These people in the yellow rainbow.

In the long walk back to town,
I hear for the last time the lamenting
Topaz hawks descending cactus by cactus,
Greeting me with evening, leaving
Me in a dome of fatigue,
With hands deep in the dust of the valley.

POEM FOR THE PEOPLE
WHO CAME FROM THE MOON

Deer meadows end where wind settles
In the city's heart of mushrooms; the river
Willows echo Snoqualmie chants to children
Chasing quail into the arms of afternoon.
Within their houses rising from the sea,
Carriers of the dream wheel often sing
Their rain songs to the stranger.

After the evening logs burn down to masks,
Hunters from the sky sometimes enter the spruce
Canyons of their dreams, flap like wild
Fern inside Hawk's sleeping village.

Having circled the lake for dawn,
Blue mallards land on the bow
Of a lost canoe. Elders with family
Buried under the thundering clouds
Put their ears against the rotting cedar,
Hear hoofbeats of deer and elk
Pound tributes in their veins:
The pulse of a new moon with many seasons.

A BASKET OF
THREE AVOCADOS
(for Natalie)

I see your gift of avocados ripen like summer
On top of the refrigerator.
Their green skin stops the drone
Of the leafless sky, the fog fading
The madronas, the wrinkled day that holds
Together the wind's torn kite.
These fruit are an aging poem,
Evading both definition and description:
An abstract song too lyrical to learn;
A departure from melody and self.

ASCENDING RED CEDAR MOON
(for Philip and Ann McCracken)

1

Out of friendship and a slow retreat of the blood,
I stop to watch Sun give away
Its morning names, among petroglyphs
Of spear, trap, and drum.
Streaming ocher threads over the salmon ceremony,
Rain falls in four directions.
And wind hails Grandfather at N'huia-wulsh,
After greeting the village moss, shells,
Berry and water baskets. Children
Circle the Elders in half the moon who carve
Their lives into this totemic dream.

My son has run off somewhere,
Perhaps to discover the thundering hawk,
The rainbow beauty of deer
Turning like sunlit streaks down the path.
Or maybe he is learning how to fall,
Make room for pain and the nightmare in his heart,
Rest with bear in the ear of the blizzard?
Like Niatum, his Great-great Grandfather,
He believes in bluejay's humor,
The legends in the long dives of killer whale,
Will lead him to fern-shadowed meadows,
The Elwah river's thousand year elegy to Spring.
With the gift of the blind,
He may turn these roots into song or to dance.

My sweet woman, keeper of the poem,
Floats like a waterbug,
A naked fan of sunlight.
I will lie with her soon in the soft,
Secret room of willows.

2

In Owl's light, we hold hands with the fire
And the moon spreading its feathers
Over the Ho-had-hun sky.
Now dancing in honor of the Seven Brothers,
The drums grow quiet as the river birds,
And we see First People step
From the graves of rotting white fir.
The Elders rise first in greeting;
It has been so long since the Klallams
Have heard such weeping:

"*Chee chako.*   *An-na-du!*   *An-na-du!*
Mox-pooh.   *Mox-pooh.*"

✷ *AT A FRIEND'S HOUSEBOAT*
(*for Charlotte*)

The moon drops the light of July
Like bells into the water.
Tonight we party with friends
Who are not afraid
To cross the shadows of the senses,
Imagination guiding them
Through the brilliant maze of nakedness.

The wars pass from our
Vision like planets.
By the wharf, madronas lift
Our eyes to stars
Growing sapphire, then silver
In the lake.
The wingtips of wild duck
Ride the wind like a current.

On the porch, facing the Olympics,
Our conversation harvests
Green shades from the sea;
Time rocks like a boat.
By the music's rhythm,
Walls of pretense and language
Reach for the hands
Of the sculptured clock
On the floor.

Circling our friends
With a necklace of laughter, puns,
We step outside to feel

The ocher moon flow out
Our arms: the long, the short,
The undulating shadows.

After dancing on the lake
Like moths, we sit
On the evening's blue montage.

❧ HOMAGE TO CHAGALL

1

The candle takes the first desperate
Leap through the window, flaming a rainbow
To the black valley on the moon.

In a corner, a weary juggler feeds his heart
This star; then decides to tumble
Inside the blue cow's crystal ball,

Seven songs, circling night and day.
He is joyous, and no one thinks this strange;
Besides, the town has stopped the rage

For burying their lies in the goat's footprints.
Quite happy for a moment, the synagogue
Crier trades songs for spring rain.

Sleepy children on their way to school
Watch the bearded violinist strand music
On the poplar trees; laughing, the green rabbi

Puns the Czar in Hebrew: for decades, police
Have rolled off the ghetto wall like dice.

2

And his love for woman is a peacock's dance
At sunset. Like Redon, Monet, Picasso,
He masters her lean curves along the body

Of the dream, where Eros hails painter and
          magician.
After catching the blossom from the "Sun At Poros,"
Our bodies turn into reeds, our eyes into nomads.

❧ ELEGY FOR LOUISE BOGAN

Now that you have darkened
Like a February rose,
Stark and blue with snowflakes,
Breathing the air of stone—

I'll close my eyes and ears
To the sound of moth and sparrow,
And weep for our children's loss—
Your eyes shut from yellow light.

THE CALLIGRAPHY OF THOUGHT

March rains
Speak too much of the empty rooms,
A poem of beads.

The ritual
Of the storm
Unnerves even the cat
Who runs under the bed
To hide from the ghost
Inside my head.

The four
Burlap walls, a green
Lake of swallows,
Matisse the light with nude
Women who give
No comfort.

My desire
Still searches in the dark
For the lips
Of the woman
Who fled.

The wind
Draws my face
On the windowpane.
The idea
Of tomorrow
Breaking through this night
Stammers slowly out.

I am a rock
At the willow's edge;
I break into glass.

AT THE FIRST OF FOUR PATHS TO THE HOHOKAM RUINS

(*for Barbara, a painter who showed me her way*)

1 PAST

The earth dims to a whirr of insects;
Our fears step back into the patterns of heat
While horned toads catch desert's ocher time.

Learning to breathe in cactus miles, we meet
A magpie that rises to greet the tiny suns
As if tossed by an ancient potter.

As flies weave in and out of our vision,
A lizard darts along the powdered earth,
Silence's shy guardian.

2 SKOAQUIK, PLACE OF SNAKES

Turquoise winds awaken coyote to the sky
    drummer,
A dove abandoning darkness to the sagebrush.
Pima artists have sung to many rattlesnakes;
Their designs run all along the horizon.

We drag our feet in the dust, circle the site,
Chant back to the howling faces,
The shattered vessels, clay figurines, human jars.

3 SHAKING THE BONES

As guests of hawk, we run our hands over
The reticent, wandering, moon-necklaced lizard
Before the evening voices call us back.

Saguaro wrens are the keepers of the language.
Here, feeling minds its own wild calm;
The banded gecko waits out the night.

It carries the legend down our spines,
Grows remote, touches us like a medicine feather.
Now and then broken pots rattle the winds home.

Vibrating gold, fading with the village grave,
The sun burns away the earth before our eyes.
We close them and feel hawk turn snake
Over to his rainbow side.

❧ *POEM IN DECEMBER*

Running through streets cobbled
In crystal, heavy pines drift
Like snowy owls across our eyes.
White birds cast a black shadow
Into the heart's cold season.

The mountain wind slowly draws
The spirit of solitude
From the winter branches.
Covering our footprints, we meet
Fishermen and woodcutters,
The magicians of this village.

Turning off the main street,
A white cat traces the roundest
Cottage with bold, thin green eyes.
His cool stare of indifference
Marks him as an expert of December
Refugees, occasional strangers
Who may wander past his last impressions.

Under the hard-edge blue
Evening, a priest plays
The mysteries of memory,
The longings of the blood,
For the old white cat in the window.
The three of us reach to catch
A leaf of the moon falling
On the stone steps.

Following the pebble voices
Of children scattering snowbirds
From the tower, we are ready to lie
Down in exhaustion, sleep
In the remains of our thirteen bodies.

LEARNING RESOURCES CENTER
IMMACULATE HIGH SCHOOL
803 TERRY AVENUE
SEATTLE, WASHINGTON 98104

❧ ODE TO A GENERATION

The deliriums of our city,
Blue wreckage in a sea of flesh and steel,
Leave me watching swallows close
The bridge of my eyes with stark maps.
Who knows the way to silence anymore,
The life of the stone or the reed?

Today we see our naked bodies
As poems to the tradition of lovers.
The pulse of their breasts and loins
Echo the only human history
We care to remember, call our own.
Our strength flows from the sweat of love.

Aging photographs drew us through
The hallways of our fathers,
Into the secret books, longing of our mothers,
Who found their own way past
The darkness of freeways and police,
The white emptiness of youth.

We discover no more in the parks,
The bars, the parties, the bedrooms,
Than what they whispered to each other
In the final years of their green dance,
When the parties drove them home again,
To the man or woman, lost or found.

For years a boy listened to the walls
Of faces from the tiny room beyond,
Heard conversations repeat the music

In which he played no part.
But when he did fall off to sleep,
White horses pranced on joyous, yellow sands.

She had little trouble growing shy
Of the world in which she found herself.
There were puzzles, jump rope, and books
To mirror her hopscotch fantasies.
O she cried into the walls of grief,
Many times, but never, never stopped the dream.

So now, laughing when we can, feeling
Our way through the urine yellow streets,
To the room with a lake of lilies,
We close the door without looking back.
In 6 a.m. light, the wrens roosting
Near the window of our bedroom waken our cells
By sun rays, blossoming into song.

FRIENDS AT THE LAKE

1

I watch her from a distance,
Know she seeks moon's new beginning,
The broad leaf that will seal off
Memory, the violent accident—
Her lover calling this solitude
The beautiful artist in his life.

The colors of the moon return
In the waves of her hair. On the shore,
She buries old sorrows in the reeds,
Her song answering the teal
Growing mute in the violet grass.

Can I meet her courage with reserve,
Take her with me in my mind
When I leave soon?

2

Her house is a chant, a quiet bloom
Of yellow, orange, vermilion,
A field of rose, chrysanthemum, hyacinth.

When speaking of her son, her voice
Rests in the room of darkness,
Follows his laughter all the way to Spring.

3

Her eyes in the candlelight
Speak to me of sexual play and my own
Longing. We retreat, though I wish

To embrace her loneliness,
Hold her close until our loins
Move like creatures with the land.

4
Sitting across from her,
I vanish in the cottage of her smile.

If we grow into love, I will enter
Her like a grateful gypsy.
Now, she is my faith in woman;
I am settling like water over stone.

AFTER CONSULTING AN ELDER POET ON AN ANTI-WAR POEM
(*for Elizabeth Bishop*)

You said to me today,
"There's nothing you can do,"
And spoke of Auden's line:
"Poetry makes nothing happen."
And though I honor you,
And see you stare at the fish,
An object you tipped toward light,
And then, left in a rainbow,
Let slip back into the sea,
I'll tell you dying into self,
A sweet woman's white caress,
The mirrors of a hundred books
Have failed to bring to me:

It was Socrates who said
To his Athenian friends,
That governments are only
Governments with many heads
That cannot think as one.
History shows how they swing
From war to peace and back
Again, in one wide sweep
Just as the pendulum
Of European clocks
That one can see return
The towns to silent years.

If the ash of each new war
That settles in our bones,
And deadens us in youth,

Is no more than a negative
Of the Kennedys and King,
Has no more weight than what
We felt the day the Apollo
Spaceship landed on the moon,
And Auden's line is true,
Then why are you, or I,
Still living with the dark,
Singing out the ruins?

❧ THE SIXTIES, NO. 1

A decade ago this city Klallam returned,
His faded thoughts shook the dreamer's bones;
Black dotted dice clicked with the heated game.
Looking back that far with wide open eyes,
He hears the snowball crack the ghetto window.
In the long leaf sun, June grew corn and cherries
And he was quick to harvest summer's field.
Differences of sky settled the way autumn
Drew him closer to the ocean rose
Wrapped in her green vine, thin thorns of hope—
And the robin and cat flew and chased about
Through his drunken mind as he slept in jail.
Children born in war torn streets will choose
Their loves, their hopes, and what to fear of death.

A sailor drunk on moondust from the sea hears
In a sweat and bruise bar, a man beats the demons
From the dance, when his woman feels happy
    naked.
Alone, the vision is a blue snake curling
Round his tall and very empty glass:
Raven, trapped in the bar's drunken mirror,
Springs open the magical box, letting him taste
No blood just when he wonders with an error
Splitting face where he could fall with a harder
Thud. The crowd laughs to the tickled clock.
And moon says nothing about the preference of
    pain
To August's deceit. Rattled by shaman vanity,
He follows Raven's laughter through the broken
    door.

The women, art, and bars sink to the bottom of his
     eyes;
The sea he's left rolls him into the pilings once
     more.
On the dock, his desire is a silent pulse of rain;
The early morning escapes like a faint train whistle.
He takes a taxi down every street, mapping out his
     soul;
Sighting Trickster, whom he never loses, he
     pretends
Indifference. Yet, his smile fades, as if he saw
A stranger ghost. The driver says don't worry,
     wrecks
Are common on this road. It takes one leap, three
     falls,
And a song to reach his door. He tries to believe
That when the last woman left, and he cut the rose
Bush down, the moon seemed less ugly. At his
     cottage,
With head between pillows, he sees Soul-catcher
     edit
His manic history, starting from accumulated ash.

Noon, the next day. Eyes droop like an old
    herring's.
A hunger ended with the first white leaf cold.
Seattle. They howled all night for the love of their
    loins.
Their hearts grow cool only in blood-maced streets.
Insomnia ran up the bedroom wall like an
    inkblot—
The mouse in the trap caught the cat at the hole,
The cricket in the wall said the city would fall:
A clack of brick collapsing in a tidal wave.
What comfort can they find in their parents' books?
His Indian ancestors never reached the island;
His father sang Irish drinking songs till he
    drowned;
Her Swedish-German parents remember nothing.
Hoping Eros guides the fools through the maze,
They create their own mythology in bed.

WHERE THE DEAD ENDURE,
THE LIVING SING

1 TOTEM

Mother spruce hid me from my ancestors,
Myself, friends, enemies,
Coyote laughing like the cliff.
In the black footprints of the moon,
I was the dream's arrow.

Lying beneath its rotting scars,
I heard the Fire Dancers,
Burning their songs into the late afternoon,
A shaman rattling out wolf's calling
For youth's green death.

2 TO *O-le-man*

There are nights when Old Man
Is the crier for The Moon of Changing
Seasons, a reed for wind and loon.
And at sunrise, he will throw his net
Into the Elwah river that pools
Many ways for salmon. At such an hour,
Chickadee and dragonfly feed
In the silent offerings of pine.
It is then I run for coyote's new shield.

3 VILLAGE AT NEAH BAY

The Makahs gather each summer to let
Old Heart loose again,
Rainbow the cape with fires,
Feast on salmon, wine, and *tuk.*
Somehow they are happy while the sea
Carves their paddles into grains of white sand,
Carries them away on the tide.

As the sun cools in the breakers of evening,
Drums strike not a chord in the heart
Of Raven, but give a myth
To the children, the whale hunt
When their fathers roamed the coast for days,
And like tonight, draw those left
To hurdle their griefs on the fires, live
In the jaws of shell and bone.

❧ TO YOUR QUESTION

1

The day you appeared I began to speak
More gently to the woman lying in my field.
Your smile penetrated my nightmare
Like the faint cry of a sparrow.
You turned, your eyes were warm as feathers.
Again, I was shamed by my bitterness, exile.

2

I write this brief poem because your world
Is your family's and is new to me,
And to tell you poets sing to themselves
What they long to write to you.
The wind measures the counterpoint to frost,
Scattering maple leaves like a fugue.

3

The shimmering image of your body lingers
As shadows from the lake, breaking
In the dawn fiction. I touch from memory
Your delicate thin hands, holding
Them like a gift from the blind.
I am trying to understand your fear that we
Might be singing for two different moons.

After the third time around, I step toward
The street and home, wondering if the lake's
Green mirror and the morning will cross
The landscape of your question, open your blossom
To the sun, blazing in the cattails.

❧ CROW'S COTTAGE

Stranding the four walls together like beads,
He sits at the desk, while silence dreams of raiding
A nunnery. Before him hangs a Woman with child;
It drifts off in her arms, at her breasts.
On the left, a gypsy woman with violin steps closer;
As wind's red dancer she whirls past
The men clapping from the gold-heavy strokes.
Above the candle on the book pile, sky
Reads patiently the seven tales of incense.
Under its hovering wingtip, birch leaves, stars,
And moth, hide out, far from home.
By the window, with face in the sand, a bull
Cuts a strange grace, a sword pinning its soul to
      the dead.
Flowing from the woody eyes of the crowd,
Blood rips off the mask of grief, the black muscles
Of the Toro de Lidia, the thin arms of youth
Cheering from the street, the hands of the artist
Who sees foam on every creature's mouth.
He hears mirror crash into white whispers.

𝕥 *THE CLOWN*

Night crawls
Over the sleeping eyelids
Of Seattle
Like a centipede.

When the pock-marked
Star falls into the white
Harbor without causing
One other person to feel
A wish caught in his throat,
I take three leaping
Zigs and a zag through the crowd,
Realizing the strange
Fool running down the silence
Is me chasing my ghost.

I drift along
Tomorrow's avenue
Like a runaway balloon man,
Trying to find
The woman who sang
The summer's dying song.

The Space Needle
Rises to the godless heavens
Like a thin hollow tomb
For astronauts.

Chasing the years
Back up the tower steps
To where each

Window shows the flight
Of one more animal—
Memory breaks,
Rattling my soul,
A marble pinging its
Way back down
The tower
Spire.

Shaking the droning sea
From my eyes,
I fall out of my shadow,
Now, a dancing bear,
A totem to face the streets.

✲ THE MAN STILL CHANTS
   FOR HER

The night climbs down into the corner of my eye.
Did I see you doing your ugly dance again,
For Jack on the street and Bob in a row? The black
Wind laughs; the wires hiss. You're up to your
    tricks;
Rub snow back and forth across my face. I don't
See you that comical. Yet, try to stay calm. You
Might be this night's Trickster, but I'm beginning
To leave you for the dark. If you step back into
    your
Feathers, I'll step back into mine. At least we know
It's even odds from now on. I feel like pulling you
Out of my heart with your own claw. Remember
    our fern
Bed that we often rode until our skin felt touched
By the moon? I'd damn near chase you just for
    that,
But it's not my way. And we traded far too many
    scars.

❧ *ELEGY FOR VERNON WATKINS*

He came to our pine cone city of rain
To help us find the way to praise
White blossoms, nightmares, and the sea.

And by making the wave's breath our own,
Show us how to live with violence and the rose.
Then, as if no longer caring to out-rhyme death,

He left us like a hawk falling from a vermilion
Sky, turning away the light, abandoning the known.

FOR MY FRIENDS
LIVING ALONG THE
WALLA WALLA RIVER:
Dale, Kathy, and Shona

Yes, you've seen the wars inside my head.
I am the carrier of wind's broken shields,
Always fearing to close my eyes; see the explosion.
Yet, upon reaching your home, I wanted to call
To the mountains. And the Moon of Deep Snow
In the undulating spruce nearly brought me to
    tears;
A blind wolf weeping. I am nightmare's
Escaped beggar; it can't be helped. Those children
In Asia have eyes, hair, lips that mirror
My son's. Their faces are familiar, their red
Eyes have been as white as Shona's, your beautiful
Daughter's. So I am here to ask forgiveness.
For years I've been digging for the roots,
And finding songs accusing me of cowardice,
Songs breaking the wolf in my dream to stone;
But he's learned to dodge my teeth of arrows.

O my friends, I want to watch trout leap home;
Hold your hands as we search with each star
For the river's golden branch. And we can
Do this easily because your cabin is a Klallam
Longhouse embedded in the canyon's heart.

Later, chanting until morning, I hailed the spirits
Behind the rainbow fans in red moon flames.
If only this flame could burn in the city.
Often I feel my country crumble within me.
One day soon will I be found stumbling along
Some unnamed street, lost without the songs

Or the silence of the eldest shaker of ashes?
Is it a hunter's footprint tracking my youth?
Is another leader shouting orders to the troops
Charging through my sleep? And why are the
      women
Of the field fleeing me? My desire is a four
Pointed wind stopping for them. And must I,
To believe in my beloved Seattle, have
The courage to kiss the breasts of death?

O don't be afraid of my retreating mind,
Zig-zag falling to the sweet earth.
It's because you love the river, the salmon,
The stars, that I sing all night; step
Through the mud for Crow and the Grandfather
Inside me; balance my joy by my grief;
Dream owl flies in these flames; get so close
To moss and fern that I can feel their dew on my
      lips.
And may we run in circles through the valley
Until the Walla Wallas laugh at our fears, ghosts!
And may Trickster, the blood's drummer,
Mock no more my dead selves swaying home.

A JOURNEY TO GUEMES ISLAND IN AUGUST

The moon roosts like wren in our hands
When we stop picking up our fallen companions,
The scars running for the beach,
Echoing, memory is a river of lies.

Feeling good about arriving here,
We move on to celebrate the blood's dance—
Like making love on the earth no body
Remembers but coyote and the weeds.
Our nerves dig in the sand for the journey back.

She drifts beyond the highest waves
As if reflecting her grave thirst for summer.
Awed by her footsteps that keep growing fainter,
We follow her, until we are not sure
Whether she is crossing the opposite shore
To the mountain, or her song bearing
The seven-pointed wind in her beak.

Now she reaches for your hand. Take it;
When you touch the tips, your wounds
Will vanish like the body lying
Face upward, lost in the lightness of the sky.

❧ LOVE POEM

Once again, the twilight of your face,
The unknown bird in your voice,
Draws me to the green vision,

Your song about the awkward moments
Of summer, the pain of too much moonlight,
A Natalie I saw alone

At someone else's party years ago,
Where you called me to your side,
And I held my heart, cupped in my shadows,

As a dark offering to your smile,
Our soft-spoken isolation.

✻ THE TALKING WALLS

1
The day I arrowed a fist of words
Into you, despair cracked like a rib,

Dividing the night into the lost wars,
The hours we loved like cranes on the marsh,

The streets we crossed, friends discovered,
The noisy parties that left us nameless,

When we heard the retreating footsteps
Of the wounds we were last week.

2
The first autumn sent us off dancing
Right out of our clothes.

In the light of Yellow Leaf Moon,
We were one with the rhythmical blue bed.

In the shade of dogwood, rose, and wild camas,
We sang to the river and the dawn.

3
Of course, today, Crow is laughing
Up his pole, smug as a statue.

And the lovers running down the beach,
Chasing ducks and gathering shells

Blow through the windows like ghosts.
And the gold poppies we stole

From the florist disintegrate like moth
Wings caught in the broom's sweep.

Even the house cricket rubs out
Our season, dated as jazz.

❦ *IN PRAISE OF THE DARK*

1

Memp-ch-ton, totemic, feathered in snowslides,
Invites the blue-edged pines
To move us on into nakedness. Running
Beside the river, neither the rapids
Nor dragonflies call us strangers or fools;
They too have been peeled
Down to moonlight, wind, appearances.

And they know it was for pain we traveled
Back to this, that owl sits in the chaos
Of our hearts. Following night past the ferns
To a sunset, after an hourless rain,
Fear retreats into the longhouse of memory.

2

We rise from earth like geese in a white
Space. For the first time, we fall
From history, upward and unafraid.
I slip from the path with a sidestep, stop
At a clearing, close my hands around
Her supple hips, enter the first
Circle of her morning song.

She steps closer to the fire, to listen
To the popping cones shoot skyward,
Lies with me for the joy of it.
After breakfast, I read her lines
Left by snails on the broad leaves of dawn.

SLOW DANCER THAT NO
ONE HEARS BUT YOU
(after an intaglio by Kevin Cuddy)

She, the sensual creature, the green singer,
Interpreter of the moon's stone calendar,
Sweet fragrant wanderer through your forest,
Calls you with the ambivalence of the wind.
When she walks with you, the calligraphy
Of maple leaves reveal our lost histories:
The soul's abstract vagabonds.

The way her song paints the owl's white face
On the black mask of the pine hillside
Suggests her desire may be to reach the heart
From memory, trembling in its nakedness,
A bold flame dancing in the moonlit clearing.
Is not her lover one of the thin Tricksters
Moving closer? Inside, far from the sleeping

Crowd, her stare marks a serene eye of departure.
How she arrived at the beginning of sleep
Drives you on and on through the fields,
Running from shadow to shadow, toward her hand
That is never quite within reach,
But somehow encouraging, so you go on, knowing
She is what is real, important for your death.

Forever smiling, her green pupils radiate your
Hard desire, and she starts to set you free,
Brush her fingers across your soul's icon.
From now on, falling to sleep will be easier—
She has left her blue dancers in the wind,
River echoes of the women who fled.

❧ THE OPEN WINDOW

Buried under the rocking afternoon, his fears,
A cedar man dreams of carving the cave out of
     himself.
As if hearing the bluejay, resting in the shadow
Of the birch, sun hiding, he smiles. The hour snaps,
Confused about direction, who's calling. But he,
Having chosen the dreamers as his counselors,
Sees the writing on the leaf, the yellow river.
Suspicious, weary of doors leading to the past,
Windows glaring back the future, he begins to extend
Feelers from his hands, feet, awaken to the sage,
Chattering dancer of the blind. Half-heartedly,
He slaps at the fly investigating the mountains,
Bridges, valleys of his face, and rises to greet the bird
Outside, the twilight that crystallizes the fantasies,
Yet calls the scars to run for each circle of the moon.

❧ *TO PAIN*

Voices of her discarded victims stutter
Down the hall like trembling gnomes.

Here in my moth white hospital bed
I scheme for darkness to hide

Me from my new mistress, not voluptuous,
Or scented, but cool as a beautiful machine.

When the room's one light raises
Her razor clacking claws to my face,

The beasts in the brain run for color.
My arms and one good leg guard the hip

Like a starving dog his bone. Silence.
The wall around the throat is choking time.

The uniform sheet covers me like a skin.
She seduces me to numbness;

I am again free and alone.
Her arms are spidery nightmares;

Her embrace races up and down my eyelid.
I feel like a broken window;

A photo who has lost his negative.
Yet, if she drifts from my bed, just once,

I'll slip on my mask——dare the bitch
To pull me from my ether coma!

❧ *THE STORM*

1
October hails through the branches,
Dropping husks to the path like a field of rain.
A dog howls at the lightning as if the wind
Was caught in its throat. Shifting
The sea cloud collage, the Changer waits
For each heart to claim its proper fear.

2
Walking down Trickster's afternoon,
I hear small leaves of an unknown forest
Scatter like crickets caught in a blizzard;
Twigs snap like voices of old people
Left inside with a place to rock back
And forth in the windowless corner of reason.

3
Sky Juggler of the heart's glare, the dog,
The chestnut tree, my joy is bitter,
But as white as the blossom, wedged between stone.

4
All wind, rain, and rattled bone, we leave
The campus decadrone, two-thirds
Cricket, one-third leaf.

❧ POEM TO THOSE NOW
UNITED BY CANKPE OPI

Grass hides its children in cricket's earthen bowl.
These legends are simple: by noon,
Wind roams the plains like coyote.
Nothing moves in these hills but worms
Digging songs into tomorrow. Under
Twilight's black wing, howling for the red
And yellow, we dance for the moon,
Begin our search for the lost door from the wound.
Every step burns a new color into the smallest vein.
By the time women weep for the crushed
Voices of white spider on the rose, the young
And old have claimed their scars. Still,
Despair offers children running down the night,
Sweet pollen from the graves of exiled dreamers.

II

LEGENDS
OF THE MOON

*My flowers shall not perish
Nor shall my chants cease;
They spread, they scatter.*
                    —Aztec

This cycle is in memory of Mrs. Annie
Patsey Duncan, my Great-Aunt, and her
father, Young Patsey. Young Patsey's
Indian name was Niatum. My Great-Aunt
honored me with the gift of this name
three years ago. Because of this, I have
made it my last name.

✣ CENTER MOON

Wolf abandons his footprints on the face
Of Center Moon. Without food
For days, he feels his shadow branch
Out into pine boughs.
The crystal faces of wolves drift on
And on like snow through our winter sleep.
When we no longer hear them calling
To their brothers, we will wear
Their spirits like a shield.

❧ *LONG DAY MOON*

1
Passing under the vague eye of the sparrow,
Down its slow journey through nothing
But the serenity of silence,
The sun cascades into the alders' deep ravine.
A bush of red berries, dark as the afternoon,
Seems to draw the rest of the feathery
Clan to the buoyant branch.
Hearing the hours linger in the maples,
We enter fern houses like moles.

2
On leaving the path for the street,
A tiny crocus springs us into faith.
Breathing like guardian stones of ocher
Light, we turn back the vines, hope earth's
Blossom will find the passing moon.

❧ SORE EYE MOON

1
Sunning himself in the snow,
Crow dreams like a stone, willow's
Ancient companion. Is he my Grandfather?

2
The day flowing after the sun,
I stare at the bottomless river.
Wren's family skittering toward taller
Grass knows where to rest,
Why don't I, and wind?

3
The woman who sleeps in my sunlight,
My friends, those awaiting my return to the city,
Let me sink into the Hoko's reflection
Like a trout. An empty canoe in its rapids,
My violent soul roots itself to the dark.

4
Grandfather, Great-Uncle,
I chant for your help once again:
As coyote would ask the cave, is this the way
To cool my rage and fear?

5
When Sore Eye Moon tramples
Through the cedars like a bear,
I will sleep within Crow's lean shadow.

FROG'S MOON

1

We hear from frog,
Lying like a moon among the reeds,
That Black Elk is dead.
As if tipped by the flight of loon,
The river has lost its voice at dawn.

2

Quietly drifting beneath cottonwood trees,
Over the white earth of Paha Sapa,
His spirit dances as a blade of grass
In the black winds.

3

When I can sleep in the violent waters
Of my blood, I may spend many seasons roaming
These hills, stepping like wolf
Into the flaming rainbow door,
Glimpse the Lakota Elder toss pollen dust
To eagle, melt the snow from my eyes.

IDLE MOON
(for Jan, Panos and Marilyn)

The deer graze uneasily across
Moon's desert; a field
Of cranes join our dance to the lake.
What roams in the night
Tells me this summer may be motionless,
As the yellow violet.

The next time she puts her wish
Into my song, I will whisper to her
The magic colors I see flowing in her hair.

Wandering like children of the moon,
Slipping slowly into the water,
Our nude bodies desire to capture nothing;
We have tossed our poems into the sky,
The white peacock blossoming in the heart.
Even the moth resting on the lily pad
Hears our secret song,
And we its green chorus calling swallows.

❧ FULL LEAF MOON

1

It hangs like a yellow stone
Over the rippling grass of Paha Sapa.
An old evening shadow,
A meadowlark closes its eyes on late Spring.
A few Lakota ponies, grazing
Near the Powder river, seem to be watching
For the strange man of the Oglalas.
Silent, half in dream, a boy dives into the river
To find the Fathers' way.

2

Dust from the prairie moves down canyons
Of buffalo skulls like a mouse.
Climbing out the white face of a century,
A cricket, luminous as smoke,
Soft as lightning chip,
Is waking to the time of no shields.

3

At dawn, the boy runs from the hills.
Slowly, eagle closes the first yellow circle
With his fall. A voice roams the grass:
"Crazy Horse is dreaming!
Grandfather paints your past
On the shield's buffalo mirror!"
The boy kneels to the earth,
Welcomed by the song of Crazy Horse,
Humbled by the eagle feather
That sounds his passage into manhood.

RED BERRIES MOON

The evening primrose is a light child
Of mountain and sky; summer's nomad.

The falls mold riddles out of shadow,
A thousand questions out of mist;

Hidden, tricky, never really here,
Nor there, bluejay watches

For the moon to fish the river.
Pebbles roll, pass over and under the stars,

Our dreams giving way to the end.
Harvesting strawberries in the field

Of white moon, we rise to run the orchard's
Long, wing-opened memories.

❦ BLACK CHERRIES MOON:
Three poems on a wish for silence

1
Far from the rotting city,
Deep into the interior of our rainy forest,
I kneel to drink *tahoma* water and hear
Fox telling Crow Child the ways to travel rivers.

2
Buzzing around and around my face,
Mosquito would rather dance,
Than cut the solitary summer thread.

3
Soon I will rest like a branch
From the fallen cedar, a naked friend
Of the moon, servant of *polaklie*.

YELLOW LEAF MOON

There are so many legends in the pool
Of the yellow leaf circle
That we have started the evening fire
With a mound of maple, hoping
To dissolve our fear of white thunder,
The bat's ease in descending the moonless path.

❧ MOON OF CHANGING SEASONS

Floating in and out of dusk,
A girl, with hair the color of black ash,
Stops feeding the moon birds her joyous songs.
Chilling her face, tears fall
Like sparrows down her rainbow grace.

Still wandering somewhere on the prairie,
Her brother has not returned
To praise her sweet, flowing body.
Afraid to tell her father of her love,
Last night's dream of a deer
Frozen to a hunter's back, she wails
In the blizzard, near the thundering river,
Her grief buried in the knife.

❧ FROST MOON

1

Coyote's howl gives a village to Elwah river ghosts,
Red-cedar fishermen too ancient
As the ferns to settle a field of poetry,

Too buried under the rain of many faces to be
      reached
With a watch. And like the song of owl,
Dog Salmon wind carries a light

Meditation over the white fir slopes,
The path zig-zagging its way toward the town.

2

At the edge of Memp-ch-ton, he thinks of nothing
More than how a passing cloud blackens
The animals of the willow moon,

Empties out the mind's wasted images, raising
Wind's pitch one green octave above Crow
Confronting the ghostly shakers of the branch.

As if storm had changed the secret trails
Of his Klallam fathers, the stranger
Grows as mute as his tracks.
Now he walks in darkness like the Crow.

CENTER MOON'S LITTLE BROTHER

I camp in the light of the fox,
Within the singing mirror of night,
Hunt for courage to return to the voice,
Whirling my failures through the meadow
Where I watch my childhood pick
Choke cherries, the women cook salmon
On the beach, my Grandfather sing his song to deer.
When my heart centers inside the necklace
Of fires surrounding his village of white fir,
Sleeping under seven snowy blankets of changes,
I will leave Raven's cave.

✖ MOON NAMES

Center Moon: (Assiniboine) January
Long Day Moon: (Assiniboine) February
Sore Eye Moon: (Assiniboine) March
Frog's Moon: (Assiniboine) April
Idle Moon: (Assiniboine) May
Full Leaf Moon: (Assiniboine) June
Red Berries Moon: (Assiniboine) July
Black Cherries Moon: (Assiniboine) August
Yellow Leaf Moon: (Assiniboine) September
Moon of Changing Seasons: (Lakota) October
Frost Moon: (Assiniboine) November
Center Moon's Little Brother: (Assiniboine) December
Moon of Deep Snow: (Lummi) February

✤ GLOSSARY

An-na-du: A Chinook word meaning "come." The Chinook People, like the Klallam, are one of the Salishan tribes of the Northwest Coast.

Black Elk: A noted holy man of the Oglalla Sioux.

Camas: A blue lily with edible bulbs which was a staple food for many of the Salishan tribes. The name is derived from a Nootka word meaning "sweet."

Cankpe Opi: The Lakota name for Wounded Knee, South Dakota, where a band of Sioux led by Big Foot were massacred by the 7th Cavalry in 1891. Also the scene of armed confrontation between U.S. Marshals and members of the American Indian Movement in 1973.

Chee Chako: Chinook word for "newcomers."

Crazy Horse: A noted war leader of the Oglalla Lakotas, or Sioux. He was killed by the U.S. Army while in captivity at Fort Robinson, Nebraska, in 1877.

Elwah: A river in the Klallam home country.

Ho-had-hun: The Nisqually name for what are now called the Olympic Mountains.

Hohokam: A Pima word meaning "those who have vanished," referring to the extinct civilization which flourished in southern Arizona, along the Gila River, from 500 to 1200 A.D. The Pimas are said to have descended from them.

Hoko: Another Klallam river.

Kachina: Hopi spirits often represented by masked dancers in religious rituals.

Klallam: A Salishan tribe living on the Washington coast, along the Strait of Juan de Fuca. Their name means "strong people."

Komo Kulshan: The Lummi and Nooksack name for Mount Baker. It means "white shining mountain," or "great white watcher."

Lakota: The name of the western, or Teton, division of the Sioux nation.

Leschi: An early chief of the Nisqually People, executed by the Washington territorial militia after leading an unsuccessful war to regain his tribe's ancestral homeground from the white settlers.

Lummi: A Salishan tribe living on several islands in northern Puget Sound, and on the adjacent mainland.

Makah: A Wakashan tribe living in the extreme northwest corner of Washington, neighboring the Klallam. Their name means "cape people."

Memp-ch-ton: The Klallam name for Mount Olympus, in the heart of the Klallam country.

Mox-pooh: A Chinook word meaning "to lie still and then explode."

N'huia-wulsh: The Klallam name for one of their villages, now called Jamestown. The Klallam words translate as "village of white firs."

Nisqually: A Salishan tribe living near the southern end of Puget Sound.

Nooksack: A Salishan tribe living along a river which flows from Mount Baker into Puget Sound. Their name means "mountain men."

Oglalla: The name of one of the Seven Council Fires, or bands, of the Teton Sioux. Led in the latter half of the 19th century by men like Red Cloud and Crazy Horse, they fought with great tenacity and skill against the invasion of their lands by gold miners and the U.S. Army.

O-le-man: A Chinook word meaning "chief," or "strong one," or "old man."

Paha Sapa: The Lakota name for the Black Hills of South Dakota, which are sacred to them. The name itself translates as "black hills."

Polaklie: The Chinook word for "night."

Seatco: An evil spirit, or spirits, greatly feared by many of the Salishan tribes along the Washington and Oregon coasts.

Skoaquik: The Pima name for present day Snaketown, Arizona. Skoaquik was once the central village of the Hohokam culture.

Snoqualmie: A Salishan tribe living in Western Washington. Their name means "people who came from the moon."

Tehoma: A Chinook word meaning "mountain."

Tuk: A bread made by the Indians of the Northwest.

ABOUT THE AUTHOR

Duane Niatum was born in 1938 in Seattle, Washington. He is an American Indian, a member of the Klallam tribe whose ancestral lands border the Washington Coast along the Strait of Juan de Fuca. His early life was spent in Washington and California. He joined the Navy at seventeen, spending two years of his enlistment in Japan. On his return, he was graduated from the University of Washington with a B.A. in English, and afterward received his M.A. from Johns Hopkins.

Duane began writing sixteen years ago. His poetry has been influenced by his interest in both painting and music as well as by his exposure to Oriental culture. "There are parallels between American Indian and Oriental philosophies which gave me an interesting hybrid way of looking at things. I learned restraint, how to hold back, to understate both the object and the feeling for the object. This is one of the best influences I could have had. I am grateful."

The other major influence reflected in his poems is his Indian ancestry. "My roots are in the earth and sky philosophies and arts of my ancestors. As a child, my Grandfather and Great-Uncle taught me always to humble my soul before the spiritual reality of things as well as man."

Duane's poetry has previously been published in the *Chicago Review, Prairie Schooner, Northwest Review,* and many other literary journals. He has also published a book of poems, *After the Death of an Elder Klallam,* with Baleen Press. Some of his earlier poetry was published under the name of Duane McGinnis. Niatum, which was his Great-Grandfather's name, was given to him by his Great-Aunt, Mrs. Annie Patsey Duncan, in 1971. He has since made it his legal name.

EASTSIDE CATHOLIC
HIGH SCHOOL

803 TERRY AVENUE
SEATTLE, WASHINGTON 98104